Fourth of July
FIREWORKS

Fourth of July
FIREWORKS

Patrick Merrick

THE CHILD'S WORLD®, INC.

Library of Congress Cataloging-in-Publication Data
Merrick, Patrick.
Fourth of July fireworks / by Patrick Merrick.
p.   cm.
Includes index.
Summary: Briefly explains the significance of
the Fourth of July holiday, describes the origin and
meaning of its celebration with fireworks, and
discusses the making and safety aspects of fireworks.
ISBN 1-56766-640-X (lib. reinforced : alk. paper)
1. Fourth of July—Juvenile literature.
2. Fourth of July celebrations—Juvenile literature.
3. Fireworks—United States—Juvenile literature.
[1. Fourth of July. 2. Fireworks.]   I. Title.
E286.A1395   1999
394.2634—dc21   98-51661
CIP
AC

Photo Credits

© Aaron Jones Studios/Tony Stone Images: 24
© Antonia Reeve/Tony Stone Images: 2
© ARCHIVE PHOTOS/Lambert: 13
© Baldwin H. Ward/Corbis-Bettmann: 15
© Brian Stablyk/Tony Stone Images: 20
© Cheryl R. Richter: 10
© Comstock, Inc.: 30
© J.E. Glenn/TRANSPARENCIES, Inc.: 26
© Kelly Culpepper/TRANSPARENCIES, Inc.: 29
© Mark Daniels Ippilito/Comstock, Inc.: cover
© Nathan Howard: 23
© Photri, Inc.: 16
© 1998 Ron Sherman: 9, 19
© Wayne Eastep/Tony Stone Images: 6

On the cover...

Front cover: These fireworks have all burst at the same time.
Page 2: This little girl is holding a firework called a *sparkler*.

Table of Contents

As the sun sinks low in the sky, the crowd grows quiet. It has been a busy day. There has been everything from parades and speeches to picnics and baseball. However, the best part of this warm summer day is just about to begin. Finally, the night sky grows black. Then, in the darkness, a quiet pop is heard. It is quickly followed by a second pop, and then a third. All at once, the night sky is filled with beautiful colors and shapes of light. It is truly a wonderful end to the day.

This magical day is called Independence Day, and it happens every July 4. Those colorful flashes of light are the famous Independence Day fireworks!

⇐ This crowd is watching fireworks in New York.

Independence Day is a **holiday.** That means it is a special day that people celebrate with their friends and family. On Independence Day, Americans get together to remember all that is good about the United States of America and how this country got started.

These children are watching a parade on Independence Day. ⇒

Some holidays, such as Easter and Thanksgiving, are celebrated on different days every year. That is not the case with Independence Day. Americans celebrate Independence Day on July 4 every year. For that reason, many people simply call the holiday the Fourth of July.

How Was This Country Started?

Unlike many countries in the world, the United States of America is a fairly young country. About 400 years ago, people started crossing the ocean from Europe and began to live with the Native Americans who already lived here. These new arrivals were **colonists.** The American colonists were still ruled by the King of England.

This painting shows some colonists as they arrive in America. ⇒

After a while, the American colonists began to feel that the King of England was not a good king. He would make them pay money to England, but he would not listen and help them with their problems. Finally, the colonists had enough. They decided to break away from England and start their own country.

This drawing shows the colonists protesting England's Stamp Act. ⇒

A great war followed, called the **Revolutionary War.** During the war, the American colonists fought for their freedom. On July 4, 1776, the colonists came out with an official document called the **Declaration of Independence.** The country of the United States of America was born!

Do Many People Celebrate Independence Day?

Many nations celebrate their own Independence Day. Only the United States celebrates its Independence Day on July 4.

Many families have different **traditions,** or ways of doing things, when it comes to Independence Day. Some watch parades or spend the day playing games with their families. Others spend the day remembering the brave men and women who fought to keep this country free. For most people, the most exciting part of Independence Day comes when the sky is dark and we get to watch fireworks!

Many families have come to see this parade in Atlanta, Georgia. ⇒

Why Do We Have Fireworks on Independence Day?

Fireworks have been around for a long time. The early Chinese used fireworks whenever they wanted to celebrate something special. This tradition was passed down and spread throughout the world. So when the colonists wanted to celebrate their new country, they shot off fireworks. Now we shoot off fireworks every July 4 in memory of the first celebrations.

⇐ Watching sparkling fireworks like these makes many people happy.

The craft of making and setting off fireworks is called **pyrotechnics** (py–roh–TEK–niks). This is a very dangerous job. Even in today's computerized world it is still done mostly by hand. China, Europe, and the United States all have major fireworks companies.

A professional company is setting off these fireworks in Montana. ⇒

Fireworks companies are very secretive about how they make their fireworks. Even so, the basic idea has not changed for thousands of years. All you need is **gunpowder** and fire!

If you have gunpowder on the ground and you set it on fire, it burns very hot and very fast. But if you wrap gunpowder in heavy paper, it burns even faster. In fact, it burns so fast that it shoots out a jet of hot air and flies into the sky, then explodes seconds later!

If fireworks had only a single packet of gunpowder, they would not be very exciting. So fireworks makers put other chemicals into the paper wrap. The chemicals change color when heated. It takes a lot of chemicals to get all the colors and streamers that people want to see. Some of these fireworks can weigh more than 700 pounds!

How Can We Use Fireworks Safely?

Fireworks are beautiful and exciting, but they can also be very dangerous! Every year, fireworks kill some people and injure many more. In fact, because of the danger, almost half of the states have banned people from having fireworks. In these states, only professionals can light them.

A professional company set off these fireworks on top of a building. ⇒

If you live in a state that still allows people to use fireworks, there are some very important things to remember. First, always have an adult light the fireworks. Second, make sure the fireworks are only used outside, away from anything that could catch fire. Also, never aim them at someone! Finally, whether you are lighting your own fireworks or watching a professional display, never pick up a burned firework. It still may have gunpowder in it and could be very dangerous.

As long as we are careful around fireworks, they are lots of fun. We can all wait in quiet excitement on a warm Fourth of July night for one of the most beautiful of all sights—the Independence Day fireworks!

Glossary

colonists (KOL–ih–nists)
Colonists were people who came from England and Europe to live in America.

**Declaration of Independence
(deh–klayr–AY–shun of in–dee–PEN–dens)**
The Declaration of Independence is the document that first stated that the United States of America was a free country.

gunpowder (GUN–pow–der)
Gunpowder is a powder that explodes easily. Gunpowder is used to make fireworks.

holiday (HOL–lih–day)
A holiday is a special day that people celebrate every year. The Fourth of July is a holiday.

pyrotechnics (py–roh–TEK–niks)
Pyrotechnics is the craft of making and using fireworks.

Revolutionary War (reh–voh–LOO–shuh–nayr–ree WAR)
The Revolutionary War was the battle between England and the Colonies to make the United States a free country.

traditions (tra–DIH–shuns)
Traditions are ways of doing things that are passed down from year to year. Setting off fireworks on the Fourth of July is an American tradition.

Index